THE ESSENTIAL SLOW COOKER RECIPE BOOK #2020

Easy and Delicious Recipes for Every Day incl. Indian Recipes

Matthew Patterson

ISBN - 9798673323250

TABLE OF CONTENTS

Bonus: Slow Cooker Indian Recipes 84

Cooking meals every day is usually a burden, especially for those who live a very busy lifestyle. This doesn't mean that you should renounce healthy and homemade food for you and your family.

In fact, cooking from scratch and experimenting with several ingredients can still be fun and quick if you rely on a slow cooker. These are some of the best kitchen appliances available on the market, as they offer a quick and healthy way to potentially prepare any recipes with the minimum amount of fat and effort.

In this book, you will find several useful information about how to use your slow cooker and its benefits. In addition, we have chosen some of the best recipes that you can make with your slow cooker, to enhance your cooking skills, enjoy healthy food, and have fun.

From curries to puddings, there is nothing you cannot make with your slow cooker. For this reason, we have also added a bonus chapter to this book with some of the best Indian recipes you can prepare with your slow cooker

Why You Should Use a Slow Cooker

Slow cookers are particularly cheap, and they are constantly increasing in popularity. There are several reasons why many households have decided to buy one of these kitchen appliances.

First, they provide a safe and quick way to prepare all your favourite recipes. Most importantly, they do not require the use of many fats or oil to cook your food. In other words, slow cookers are one of the best accessories to improve your cooking skills.

If you are wondering whether you should buy one, here you can find all the reasons why you should try slow cooking at least once.

Cut Down Your Prep Time

One of the best things about slow cookers is that they will cut down your preparation time. The majority of recipes only require you to throw all the ingredients in the slow cooker's basket and set the cooking time and temperature.

Bye Bye Expensive Food

With your slow cooker, you won't need to buy expensive cuts of meat anymore. You will be able to achieve delicious recipes with the cheaper cuts, such as pork shoulder, chicken thighs and beef brisket.

Besides, if you are trying to reduce your weekly amount of meat, with a slow cooker you can use let meat. All your other ingredients will be permeated with the meat aroma, creating a pure explosion of delicious flavour.

Find Some Time for Yourself

Once your food is in the slow cooker and you have set the cooking method and time, you are free to go. Slow cookers can cook your food without any help from you. All you have to do is check your food every few hours, to ensure that it doesn't need more water.

Don't forget that taking the lid off your slow cooker will release some of the eat, making the cooking time longer. In other words, you want to leave your slow cooker alone as much as you can!

The Best Tips for Using Your Slow Cooker

Slow cookers offer a healthier, cheaper and low-fat way of cooking your favourite food. Most importantly, they only require a minimum effort.

If you are looking for the best ways to use your slow cooker and always achieve the perfect results, here you will find some good inspiration from the most experienced chefs.

Always Prep Your Food

Using a slow cooker is easy, and often all you have to do is to place your ingredients in it. However, there are some foods which still need to be cooked beforehand. For example, onions, some vegetables and spices may lose their flavour if you don't pay attention to the way you prepare them.

There is no fixed rule on which food you shouldn't put in your slow cooker. The best thing to do is to experiment with different ingredients and cooking methods until you find what works best for you.

Trim Fat from The Meat Before Cooking

When using your slow cooker, you don't need to add any oil because the natural moisture of your food is usually enough. For this reason, you can just get rid of the fat of your meat. This will not only make your food healthier and more delicious but will also prevent the fat from draining away and creating pools of oil in your slow cooker basket.

Reduce Liquids

Just like fat, extra liquids from your food may spoil your ingredients or leak out from the top of the slow cooker, as they may not be able to evaporate completely.

When following a recipe that you want to readapt for your slow cooker, you should use 1/3 less liquid then you would normally add to your saucepan.

Prepare Your Food the Night Before

Your slow cooker will significantly cut down your preparation time. However, you can make your life even easier by preparing everything you are going to need for your meal the night before.

Just place all the ingredients in your slow cooker dish, cover and store in your fridge. When you wake up, get the foot out of the fridge, leave it for a few minutes at room temperature, and then you are ready to turn the cooker on.

Spices Are the Answer

You don't need to use any additional oil to prepare your food with a slow cooker. Yet, you can add a bit of extra taste with the right spices.

For example, if you want to spice up your meat, you can roll it in some seasoned flour, or even some cornflour. Nevertheless, you may need to heat some spices in olive oil before putting them in your slow cooker.

Low Is Better Than High

Although you may wish to use your slow cooker to prepare your food quicker, you should always try to use the "low" setting as much as you can. Your food will benefit from gentler cooking, and this will also amplify all its flavour. Don't worry! If you are in a hurry, you can still use the high setting and your food will be delicious!

Not All the Ingredients Go Together

The majority of slow cooker recipes require all the ingredients to be placed in the basket together, so they can cook at the same time. Of course, you must know your food's cooking time, to ensure that no ingredient is undercooked or overcooked.

Nevertheless, pasta, fresh herbs and rice usually must be added toward the end of your cooking time. This will keep them "al dente" and preserve their aroma and taste. Other ingredients, such as root vegetables, usually take longer and must be added at the beginning to ensure that they cook perfectly.

Always Follow the Instructions

Slow cookers are very easy and intuitive to use, and you will fall in love with them immediately. However, you should always ready your manufacturer's manual. It contains useful guidelines on cooking times and temperatures, as well as all the information you need to use your slow cooker correctly.

Clean Your Slow Cooker

It is essential to wash your slow cooker after every use, especially if you have just cooked meat or other ingredients which can leave residues in your casserole.

You may be able to just put some parts of your slow cooker into a dishwasher, while others may need more attention. You will find all the information on how to clean your slow cooker on your manufacturer's manual.

Food That You Shouldn't Put in Your Slow Cooker

Slow cookers can be very versatile and usually allow to cook any type of food. However, there are some ingredients which should be handled differently, to ensure that they preserve their freshness and taste.

Raw Meat

The best way to enjoy meat is to brown it a little bit before proceeding with different cooking methods. If you just put raw meat into your slow cooker, you will get a bland and almost tasteless flavour.

Lean Cuts

Slow cooking is perfect for joint of meat, such as oxtail and pork shoulder, as they have a lot of delicious juice which will make all your recipes fragrant and tasty.

Leaner cuts, like chicken breast and fillet steak, will taste better if fried or grilled. As a general rule, you should always brown your meat first, to add all the extra and juicy flavour you need.

Delicate Vegetables

Hard root vegetables are the perfect food when it comes to experimenting with your slow cooker, as they usually need long to achieve the perfect texture. Your slow cooker will make them delicious and keep them chunky, retaining their original shape with no need for additional oil.

On the other hand, some vegetables, like peas, courgettes and asparagus, are usually too delicate. Putting them in the slow cooker may jeopardise their texture, making them mushier. If you still want to add them to your recipes, you can put them into the slow cooker until near the end of your food's cooking time.

Dairy Products

Dairy products are not suitable for prolonged cooking, as this causes them to separate and may spoil their taste. The best way to incorporate milk, yoghurt or cream to your recipes is to stir them in once the other ingredients have finished cooking.

This shouldn't be an issue if you are using vegetable-based beverages, such as soy or almond milk. However, it is always good to experiment until you find the best cooking way for each ingredient.

Liquid of Fatty Foods

Slow cooking retains food's moisture. This means that it isn't a good idea to put too much water or stock in this kitchen appliance. You can still cook some good stews, but you should always reduce the liquid quantity.

The same applies to wine and beer, which are used to add extra flavour to some recipes. In fact, alcohol needs to evaporate properly to taste good, and this would not be possible with slow cooking.

Seafood

Fish and seafood usually need to be cooked for a very short time. Otherwise, their taste will be destroyed, just like lean meat.

Based on some chefs' suggestions, there are some exceptions, like octopus and squid. The secret is to find the perfect cooking time.

Soft Fresh Herbs

Herbs and spices are the best way to add flavour to your food, especially if you are not using any oil. Nevertheless, soft fresh herbs should never be put into your slow cooker, as they will immediately lose their fragrant properties.

On the other hand, woody herbs like thyme and rosemary will preserve their aroma even after hours into your slow cooker.

Pasta and Rice

Pasta and rice are usually incompatible with slow cooking because they must be enjoyed "al dente". For example, if you let your spaghetti cook for hours into your slow cooker, you will only get a gloopy mess.

For this reason, you should cook your rice and pasta separately. If you want, you can still try adding them when the food cooker is almost at the end of its process, but you need to know the exact cooking time of your pasta.

Meath With Skin On

Cleaning your slow cooker after each use is very important and, luckily, it is usually a very quick and easy process. This means that you don't need to make your life harder by ending up picking pieces of skin out of your basket.

The best way to avoid it? Don't punt skin-on cuts of meat into your slow cooker. They need to be roasted or grilled, as this will also preserve their delicious texture.

Slow Cooker Quick & Easy Recipes

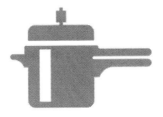

Slow Cooker Cheesy Mashed Potatoes

Difficulty: Easy ¦ Calories: 357 kcal ¦ Servings: 4
Carbs: 43 g ¦ Protein: 11 g ¦ Fat: 17 g

Ingredients

- 900 g (2 lbs.) Russet potatoes
- 55 g (2 oz.) grated cheddar cheese
- 500 ml (2 cups) chicken broth
- 2 tbsp butter
- ¼ cup heavy cream
- Salt and pepper

Preparation

1. Peel the potatoes and cut into pieces.

2. Place the potatoes chunks into the slow cooker and cover with chicken broth.

3. Cook for 8 hours (or 4 hours on high).

4. When the potatoes are ready, mash with a masher or a fork until you get your desired consistency.

5. Add butter, cheese and cream. Season with salt and pepper.

Slow Cooker Enchilada Soup

. . . .

Difficulty: Easy ¦ Calories: 338 kcal ¦ Servings: 6
Carbs: 63 g ¦ Protein: 17 g ¦ Fat: 3.5 g

Ingredients

- 150 g (1/2 cup) plain yoghurt
- 115 g (4 oz.) can diced green chillies
- 425 g (15 oz.) can whole-kernel corn
- 400 g (14 oz.) can fire-roasted diced tomatoes
- 800 g (28 oz.) can black beans
- 2 cups red enchilada sauce
- 2 cups vegetable broth
- 1 large sweet potato, diced
- ½ tsp ground cayenne
- 1 ½ tsp ground cumin
- 1 jalapeno, chopped
- 2 cloves garlic, minced
- 1 white onion, diced
- 2 tsp chilli powder
- 2 tsp fresh lime juice

- 1 tsp dried oregano
- Fresh cilantro, to garnish
- Shredded cheese, to garnish
- Tortilla chips, to serve

Preparation

1. Place all the ingredients (except for the yoghurt and lime juice) into the slow cooker.

2. Cook for 4 hours on high.

3. Place ½ cups of the soup in a blender and puree until creamy. Place back with the other ingredients.

4. Combine the yoghurt and lime juice in a small bowl.

5. Stir in the soup once it is ready.

6. Serve with tortilla chips, and garnish with fresh cilantro and shredded cheese. Add your preferred toppings.

Slow Cooker Grape Jelly Meatballs

Difficulty: Easy ¦ Calories: 310 kcal ¦ Servings: 10
Carbs: 17 g ¦ Protein: 15 g ¦ Fat: 19 g

Ingredients

- 900 g (32 oz.) frozen meatballs
- 5 cup grape jelly
- 5 cup BBQ sauce

Preparation

1. Add the meatballs to the slow cooker.

2. Top with BBQ sauce.

3. Add grape jelly and stir well.

4. Cook for about 2 hours (or 4 hours on low).

Slow Cooker Butternut Squash Soup

Difficulty: Easy ¦ Calories: 296 kcal ¦ Servings: 4
Carbs: 42 g ¦ Protein: 4 g ¦ Fat: 15 g

Ingredients

- 1 medium butternut squash, peeled and chopped
- 2 carrots, peeled
- 1 granny smith apple, chopped
- 4 cloves garlic
- 1 onion, chopped
- 1/8 tsp nutmeg

- 1/8 tsp cayenne
- 2 cups vegetable broth
- ¼ tsp turmeric
- ¾ cup unsweetened canned coconut milk
- Salt and pepper

Preparation

1. Cook the onion and garlic for 5 minutes in olive oil.

2. Add in the apple, carrots, and squash, along with all the spices. Cook for a few minutes until all the vegetables are browned.

3. Transfer all the ingredients into the slow cooker and cook for 4 hours on high, or 6 hours on low.

4. Before serving, process everything with the coconut milk in a blender until you get a smooth puree.

Slow Cooker Garlic Herb Potatoes

Difficulty: Easy ¦ Calories: 200 kcal ¦ Servings: 6
Carbs: 27 g ¦ Protein: 3 g ¦ Fat: 6 g

Ingredients

- 1.3 kg (3 lbs.) small potatoes
- 4 cloves garlic, minced
- 1 tsp dried dill
- 1 tsp dried basil

- 1 tsp dried oregano
- ¼ cup extra-virgin olive oil
- ½ lemon, juiced
- Salt and pepper

Preparation

1. Coat the inside of your slow cooker with non-stick spray or olive oil.

2. Place all the ingredients (except for the lemon juice) in the slow cooker.

3. Cook for 3 hours on high, or until the potatoes are tender.

4. Add lemon juice and serve while still hot.

Slow Cooker Easy Breakfast Casserole

Difficulty: Easy ¦ Calories: 215 kcal ¦ Servings: 12
Carbs: 11 g ¦ Protein: 8 g ¦ Fat: 15 g

Ingredients

- 225 g (1/2 lbs) ground sausage
- 1 tbsp milk
- 1 cup shredded cheese
- 6 eggs
- Salt and pepper
- 12 refrigerated crescent roll sheets

Preparation

1. Cook the sausage in olive oil over medium heat. Drain the grease.

2. Spray the casserole with non-stick cooking spray and unroll the crescent rolls into a sheet over it.

3. Spread the sausage evenly.

4. Whisk together milk, eggs, salt and pepper.

5. Pour the mixture over rolls and top with shredded cheese.

6. Cook for 4 hours (or 2 hours on high).

Slow Cooker Chai Applesauce

Difficulty: Easy ¦ Calories: 190 kcal ¦ Servings: 6
Carbs: 7 g ¦ Protein: 25 g ¦ Fat: 19 g

Ingredients

- 8 apples, chopped
- 1 cup of water
- ¼ tsp ground ginger
- ½ tsp cinnamon
- 1/8 tsp ground nutmeg
- 1/8 tsp ground cloves
- ¼ tsp ground cardamom
- 1 tsp vanilla extract
- ¼ cup brown sugar
- A pinch of salt

Preparation

1. Place all the ingredients into the slow cooker.

2. Cook for 6 hours.

3. Once ready, mash the mixture with a wooden spoon or a potato masher.

4. Let cool completely before serving.

Slow Cooker Creamy Tomato Soup

Difficulty: Easy ¦ Calories: 205 kcal ¦ Servings: 4
Carbs: 36 g ¦ Protein: 8 g ¦ Fat: 6 g

Ingredients

- 425 g (15 oz.) can tomato sauce
- 800 g (28 oz.) whole peeled plum tomatoes
- 4 cloves garlic, minced
- 1 tbsp sugar
- ¼ cup cashews
- 1 ½ cup vegetable broth
- 1 onion, diced
- ½ cup chopped basil
- 1 ½ tsp dried oregano
- Salt and pepper

Preparation

1. Place the tomato sauce, canned tomatoes, garlic, onion, broth, sugar, and oregano into the slow cooker.

2. Season with salt and pepper, and cook for 4-5 hours on high.

3. Once ready, add the tomato soup to a blender and process it until you get a creamy texture.

4. Use the same blender to puree the cashews with some water.

5. Stir the cashews cream into the tomato soup.

6. Garnish with some fresh basil and serve while hot.

Slow Cooker Breakfast Burritos

Difficulty: Medium ¦ Calories: 268 kcal ¦ Servings: 8 burritos
Carbs: 30 g ¦ Protein: 25 g ¦ Fat: 39 g

Ingredients

- 425 g (15 oz.) black beans
- 425 g (15 oz.) tofu, crumbled
- ½ cup of water
- 1 cup of salsa
- ¼ cup scallions, chopped
- ½ tsp smoked paprika
- ¼ tsp ground cumin
- ½ tsp ground turmeric
- ¼ tsp chilli powder
- 1 green pepper, chopped
- 3 cups spinach leaves
- Salt and pepper
- 8 tortillas
- Your choice of toppings

Preparation

1. Place the tofu, black beans, green pepper, scallion, salsa, water and all the spices in the slow cooker. Season with salt and pepper.

2. Cook for 6 hours on low.

3. Stir in the spinach when ready to serve.

4. Make sure you get rid of any extra liquid, then place one scoop of this mixture on the centre of each burrito.

5. Top with all the toppings of your choice and roll up the burrito.

Slow Cooker Red Beans and Rice

Difficulty: Medium ¦ Calories: 175 kcal ¦ Servings: 4
Carbs: 33 g ¦ Protein: 9 g ¦ Fat: 1.2 g

Ingredients

- 2 x 425 g (15 oz.) kidney beans
- 3 cloves garlic, minced
- 1 onion, chopped
- 1 green pepper, chopped
- 1 bay leaf
- 2 cup vegetable broth
- 1 cup of rice
- ¼ tsp cayenne pepper
- 1 tsp smoked paprika
- 2 tsp dried thyme
- 1 cup celery, chopped

Preparation

1. Place all the ingredients (except for the rice) in the slow cooker.

2. Cook for 4 hours on low.

3. When ready, stir in the rice and season with salt and pepper.

4. Cook for another 2 hours on high.

Slow Cooker Mushrooms with Ricotta and Pesto

Difficulty: Easy ¦ Calories: 400 kcal ¦ Servings: 4
Carbs: 2 g ¦ Protein: 19 g ¦ Fat: 34 g

Ingredients

- 16 medium chestnut mushrooms
- 2 tbsp green pesto
- 250 g (8 oz.) ricotta
- 25 (0.8 oz.) freshly grated parmesan
- 2 garlic cloves
- 5 tbsp extra-virgin olive oil
- Fresh parsley, chopped

Preparation

1. Place the sliced mushrooms in one layer into your slow cooker.

2. Brush the mushroom with olive oil.

3. In a bowl, mix the pesto, ricotta and garlic. Spoon this mixture into your mushrooms.

4. Cook for 8 hours on low.

5. Serve with additional fresh pesto, grated parmesan and fresh parsley.

Slow Cooker Chilli con Carne

Difficulty: Easy ¦ Calories: 820 kcal ¦ Servings: 4
Carbs: 59 g ¦ Protein: 75 g ¦ Fat: 34 g

Ingredients

- 400 g (14 oz.) can chopped tomato
- 1 kg (2.20 lbs.) lean minced beef
- 3 large garlic cloves
- 2 large red peppers, cut into chunks
- 3 x 400 g (14 oz.) cans red kidney beans, drained
- 2 large onions, sliced
- 10 sundried tomatoes
- 2 tsp dried oregano
- 2 tsp ground cumin
- 2 beef stock cubes
- 2 tbsp mild chilli powder
- 2 tbsp olive oil

Preparation

1. Fry the onions in olive oil. Stir in the garlic, oregano and all the spices.

2. Add beef mince gradually and cook until browned.

3. Stir in the tomatoes, the stock and ½ can of water.

4. Transfer everything into the slow cooker with the remaining ingredients and cook for 8 hours on low.

Slow Cooker Breakfast Yoghurt

Difficulty: Easy ¦ Calories: 120 kcal ¦ Servings: 2 litres
Carbs: 11 g ¦ Protein: 8 g ¦ Fat: 5 g

Ingredients

- 100 ml (0.4 cups) yoghurt
- 2 l (8.5 cups) whole milk
- Your choice of toppings, to serve

Preparation

1. Pour the milk into the slow cooker.

2. Cook for a couple of hours and allow to rest for another 2 hours.

3. Mix the warm milk with the yoghurt.

4. Pour the mixture back in the slow cooker and leave to rest for 12 hours.

5. Serve with porridge, fresh fruit, or your choice of toppings.

Slow Cooker Spinach and Artichoke Dip

Difficulty: Easy ¦ Calories: 182 kcal ¦ Servings: 12
Carbs: 26 g ¦ Protein: 38 g ¦ Fat: 12 g

Ingredients

- 280 g (10 oz.) baby spinach
- 125 ml (½ cup) sour cream
- 425 g (15 oz.) can quartered artichoke hearts
- ¼ cup crumbled goat cheese
- ¾ cup shredded Parmesan cheese
- ¼ tsp red pepper flakes
- 225 g (8 oz.) whipped cream cheese

Preparation

1. Wash and chop the baby spinach.

2. Drain and chop the artichoke hearts.

3. Add all ingredients to the slow cooker and cook for 2 hours, or until the cheese is completely melted.

4. Stir well and let sit for 15 minutes before serving.

Slow Cooker Apple, Pear and Cherry Compote

Difficulty: Easy ¦ Calories: 199 kcal ¦ Servings: 12
Carbs: 51 g ¦ Protein: 1 g ¦ Fat: 1 g

Ingredients

- 4 Bramley apples, cut into chunks
- 8 small apples, cut into chunks
- 8 pears, sliced
- 280 g (10 oz.) dried sour cherries
- 6 tbsp sugar

Preparation

1. Put the fruit and sugar into the slow cooker with some water.
2. Stir well.
3. Cook for 8 hours on low, or until the apples are tender.
4. If you want, you can mash the fruit until you get a thick texture before serving.

Slow Cooker Turkish Breakfast Eggs

Difficulty: Easy ¦ Calories: 165 kcal ¦ Servings: 4
Carbs: 8 g ¦ Protein: 9 g ¦ Fat:8 g

Ingredients

- 8 cherry tomatoes
- 4 eggs
- 1 small red chilli
- 2 onions, sliced
- 1 tbsp olive oil

- 2 tbsp skimmed milk
- 1 red pepper, sliced
- 1 slice sourdough bread
- 4 tbsp natural yoghurt
- Fresh parsley, chopped

Preparation

1. Grease the inside of the slow cooker with some oil.

2. Cook the pepper, onions and chilli in the remaining oil.

3. Transfer everything into the slow cooker along with the bread and cherry tomatoes.

4. Whisk the eggs with the milk and pour over the tomatoes.

5. Cook for 6 hours on low.

6. Serve with yoghurt.

Slow Cooker Delicious Meals

Slow Cooker Turkey Breast

Difficulty: Easy ¦ Calories: 182 kcal ¦ Servings: 8
Carbs: 6 g ¦ Protein: 33 g ¦ Fat: 2 g

Ingredients

- 1.4 kg (3 lbs) boneless turkey breast
- 1 sweet onion
- ¼ cup cornstarch
- 2 cups turkey or chicken broth
- ¼ cup cornstarch

Preparation

1. Place the turkey breast into the slow cooker and cover with turkey or chicken broth.

2. Cut onion into rings and add to the slow cooker.

3. Add minced garlic.

4. Cook for 8 hours on low.

5. When ready, leave to rest while making the gravy.

6. To prepare the gravy, transfer all liquid from slow cooker into a small saucepan.

7. Add the cornstarch and some water, and whisk until you obtain a smooth and thick mixture.

8. Bring to boil and keep whisking until fully thickened.

9. Serve the sliced turkey with gravy.

Slow Cooker Minestrone Soup

Difficulty: Easy ¦ Calories: 348 kcal ¦ Servings: 6
Carbs: 52 g ¦ Protein: 14 g ¦ Fat: 10 g

Ingredients

- 1 zucchini, chopped
- ¾ cup orzo pasta
- 800 g (28 oz.) diced tomatoes
- 425 g (15 oz.) can kidney beans
- 1 onion, diced
- 3 celery stalks, diced
- 3 carrots, diced
- 4 cloves garlic, minced
- ¼ cup olive oil
- 5 cups vegetable broth
- 1 tsp dried thyme
- 2 bay leaves
- ½ lemon, juiced
- 1 cup green lentils
- 1 ½ tsp smoked paprika
- 1 ½ tsp dried basil
- 1 ½ tsp dried oregano
- ½ cup chopped parsley

- Grated parmesan, to serve

Preparation

1. Cook the carrots, onion and celery in olive oil until they are soft. Add the garlic and then transfer everything into the slow cooker.

2. Add paprika, thyme, oregano, basil, broth, kidney beans, tomatoes, bay leaves and zucchini.

3. Cook on high for 4 hours.

4. Once ready, add in the dried orzo and stir well.

5. Cook for another hour, and make sure that the orzo is tender.

6. Before serving, stir in the parsley and lemon juice.

7. Top with parmesan cheese and serve into bowls.

Slow Cooker Lentil Lasagna Soup

Difficulty: Easy ¦ Calories: 386 kcal ¦ Servings: 6
Carbs: 24 g ¦ Protein: 32 g ¦ Fat: 42 g

Ingredients

- 6 sheets lasagna noodles
- 800 g (28 oz.) crushed tomatoes
- 425 g (15 oz.) can diced tomatoes
- 1 tbsp tomato paste
- ½ cup ricotta cheese
- 1 cup chopped white onion
- 1 cup chopped carrots
- 1 cup chopped zucchini
- 1 tbsp dried oregano
- 1 tbsp dried basil
- 4 cups vegetable broth
- 4 garlic cloves
- 1 cup lentils
- Chopped basil, for garnish

Preparation

1. Cook the onion until softened in olive oil.

2. Add in the carrots, zucchini, basil, oregano and garlic cloves and cook for 5 more minutes.

3. Transfer this mixture into your slow cooker.

4. Add in the canned tomatoes, tomato paste, broth, and lentils.

5. Cook on high for 4 hours, or until lentils are tender.

6. Break the lasagna sheets into pieces and add to the mixture. Cook until al dente.

7. Divide the mixture into 6 bowls.

8. Top with fresh basil and ricotta cheese before serving.

Slow Cooker Cheesy Buffalo Chicken Pasta

Difficulty: Easy ¦ Calories: 648 kcal ¦ Servings: 6
Carbs: 62 g ¦ Protein: 43 g ¦ Fat: 24 g

Ingredients

- 700 g (1 ½ lb.) boneless skinless chicken
- 450 g (16 oz.) linguine noodles
- ¼ tsp celery salt
- ½ tsp garlic powder
- 1 tbsp ranch dressing mix
- 3 cups chicken broth
- 1 tbsp cornstarch
- 1 cup shredded cheddar cheese
- 225 g (8 oz.) cream cheese
- Chopped cilantro, for garnish
- Salt and pepper

Preparation

1. Place the chicken into the slow cooker. Cover with broth and ¼ cup of buffalo sauce. Season with salt and pepper.

2. Top with shredded cheese and cream cheese.

3. Cook for 8 hours (or 4 hours on high).

4. When the chicken is fully cooked. Transfer it into a serving plate. Season with the remaining buffalo sauce.

5. To prepare the rest of the recipe, start by whisking together the cornstarch and water.

6. Shred the chicken with two forks and mix the meat with the cornstarch mixture. Combine until you get a smooth mixture.

7. Cook the noodles and serve with the chicken mixture.

8. Serve with fresh cilantro.

Slow Cooker Tailgate Chilli

. . . .

Difficulty: Easy ¦ Calories: 257 kcal ¦ Servings: 8
Carbs: 3 g ¦ Protein: 21 g ¦ Fat: 18 g

Ingredients

- 450 g (1 lb.) ground beef
- 450 g (1 lb.) ground pork
- 2 tsp cumin
- 1 tsp onion powder
- 1 tsp roasted garlic powder
- 2 cans fire-roasted crushed tomatoes

- 1 tbsp chilli powder
- 1 tsp chilli powder
- 1 tbsp chocolate powder
- 1 tsp cilantro
- 250 ml (1 cup) beer

Preparation

1. Cook the ground pork and beef until browned.

2. Transfer to slow cooker.

3. Add all the remaining ingredients.

4. Cook for 6 hours (or 4 hours on high).

Slow Cooker Veggie Korma

Difficulty: Easy ¦ Calories: 257 kcal ¦ Servings: 4
Carbs: 31 g ¦ Protein: 10 g ¦ Fat: 11 g

Ingredients

- 200 ml (0.8 cups) yoghurt
- 500 ml (2 cups) vegetable stock
- 800 g (28 oz.) mixed vegetables
- 2 tsp ground cumin
- 2 tsp ground coriander
- 1 tbsp vegetable oil
- 3 cardamom pods
- 1 onion, chopped
- 200 g (7 oz.) frozen peas
- A piece of ginger, chopped
- 1 garlic clove
- 1 green chilli, chopped
- ½ tsp ground turmeric
- 2 tbsp ground almonds (optional)

Preparation

1. Cook the onions and all of the dry spices in olive oil in a frying pan, for 5 minutes.

2. Stir in the garlic, chilli and ginger.

3. Transfer everything into the slow cooker.

4. Add the vegetables and the stock.

5. Cook on 4 hours on low.

6. When it's ready, stir in the yoghurt, peas, and ground almonds (optional).

7. Season with salt and pepper and stand for a few minutes before serving.

Slow Cooker Prawn, Pea, and Tomato Curry

Difficulty: Easy ¦ Calories: 236 kcal ¦ Servings: 4
Carbs: 18 g ¦ Protein: 24 g ¦ Fat: 1 g

Ingredients

- 400 g (14 oz.) shelled raw king prawn
- 6 garlic cloves
- 2 onions, cut into wedges
- 250 g (8.8 oz.) frozen pea
- 6 ripe tomatoes, cut into wedges
- 3 tbsp curry paste
- Fresh root ginger, chopped
- Fresh coriander leaves, chopped
- Basmati rice, to serve

Preparation

1. Fry the onions over medium heat. Stir in the tomato mix and half of the tomato wedges.

2. Whizz half of the tomato wedges in a food processor, along with garlic, curry paste, and ginger.

3. Mix in the prawns into the saucepan.

4. Transfer everything into the slow cooker. Cook for 3 hours on high.

5. Add the prawns and peas and cook for another ½ hour.

6. Serve with coriander leaves and basmati rice.

Slow Cooker Cottage Pie

....

Difficulty: Easy ¦ Calories: 600 kcal ¦ Servings: 10
Carbs: 40 g ¦ Protein: 37 g ¦ Fat: 34 g

Ingredients

- 3 carrots, chopped
- 2 onions, chopped
- 1 ¼ kg (2.7 lbs.) beef mince
- 850 ml (3.6 cups) beef stock
- 3 tbsp plain flour
- 2 celery sticks, chopped

- 1 tbsp tomato puree
- 2 garlic cloves
- 3 tbsp olive oil
- 4 tbsp Worcestershire sauce
- 2 bay leaves
- 2 thyme sprigs

For the Mash

- 1.8 kg (3.9 lbs.) potatoes, chopped
- 200 g (7 oz.) cheddar, grated
- 25 g (0.9 oz.) butter
- 225 ml (0.9 cups) milk
- Freshly grated nutmeg (optional)

Preparation

1. Brown the beef mince in a saucepan over medium heat.

2. Transfer into the slow cooker along with the puree, stock, wine, flour, vegetables, Worcestershire sauce, herbs and seasoning.

3. Cook for 5 hours on high.

4. To make the mash, cook the potatoes in salted boiling water.

5. Once ready, allow to try for a few minutes. Mash with milk, butter and some cheddar cheese. Season with nutmeg (optional), salt and pepper. Cook in the oven at 220 C (440 F) for 30 minutes.

6. Sprinkle the hot mash with more cheese and serve with the beef.

Slow Cooker Chicken, Bacon and Potato Stew

Difficulty: Easy ¦ Calories: 284 kcal ¦ Servings: 6
Carbs: 12 g ¦ Protein: 2 g ¦ Fat: 13 g

Ingredients

- 12 smoked streaky bacon, chopped
- 350 g (12.3 oz.) baby new potatoes, halved
- 500 ml (2 cups) chicken stock
- 200 ml (0.8 cups) white wine
- 280 ml (1.2 cups) pot buttermilk

- 200 g (7 oz.) shallot
- 6 skinless, bone-in chicken thighs
- 1 tbsp olive oil
- 2 tbsp tarragon, chopped
- 2 thyme sprigs
- The juice of 1 lemon

Preparation

1. Brown the chicken thighs in a saucepan.

2. Set aside and use the same oil and saucepan to brown the shallots.

3. Transfer everything (except for the lemon juice, 1 tbsp tarragon and the buttermilk) into the slow cooker. Cook for 6 hours on high.

4. Once ready, pour additional buttermilk if you want to make the sauce smoother.

5. Season with lemon juice, tarragon, salt and pepper before serving.

Slow Cooker Sweetcorn Smoked Haddock Chowder

Difficulty: Easy ¦ Calories: 550 kcal ¦ Servings: 2
Carbs: 59 g ¦ Protein: 47 g ¦ Fat: 16 g

Ingredients

- 350 g potatoes (12.3 oz.), cut into cubes
- 500 ml (2 cups) milk
- 300 g (10.6 oz.) frozen smoked haddock fillets
- 2 rashers of streaky bacon, chopped
- 140 g (5) frozen sweetcorn
- 1 onion, chopped
- Knob of butter
- Chopped parsley, to serve

Preparation

1. Fry the bacon with the butter in a large saucepan.
2. Add the onion, the potatoes and the milk.
3. Bring to the boil and then simmer for a few minutes.
4. Transfer everything into the slow cooker.
5. Cover with more milk and cook for 3 hours on high.
6. Add the fish and the sweetcorn, and cook for another 30 minutes.

Slow Cooker Irish Stew

Difficulty: Easy ¦ Calories: 673 kcal ¦ Servings: 6
Carbs: 40 g ¦ Protein: 40 g ¦ Fat: 39 g

Ingredients

- 900 g (31.7 oz.) stewing lamb, cut into chunks
- 3 onions, sliced
- 200 g (7 oz.) smoked streaky bacon, cut into chunks
- 5 carrots, cut into chunks
- 1 tbsp sunflower oil
- 700 ml (3 cups) lamb or beef stock
- 85 g (3 oz.) pearl barley
- 6 medium potatoes, cut into chunks
- 1 large leek, cut into chunks
- A small bunch of thyme
- A small know of butter

Preparation

1. Sizzle the bacon in a small saucepan, then add the lamb.

2. Transfer the meat into the slow cooker, along with onions, carrots, stock, potatoes, thyme and bay leaves. Cover with water.

3. Cook for 7 hours on low.

4. Stir in the leek and the pearl barley, and cook for another hour on high.

5. Add in the butter and season with salt and pepper before serving.

Slow Cooker Chicken Soup

Difficulty: Easy ¦ Calories: 352 kcal ¦ Servings: 6
Carbs: 4 g ¦ Protein: 35 g ¦ Fat: 21 g

Ingredients

- 2 l (8.4 cups) chicken stock
- 2 celery sticks, chopped
- 1 onion, chopped
- 2 leeks, sliced
- 2 carrots, chopped
- 1 lemon, juiced
- 1 whole medium chicken
- 1 bay leaf
- 3 thyme sprigs
- A small bunch of dill or parsley, chopped
- Crusty bread, to serve

Preparation

1. Place the onion, carrots, celery and leeks into the slow cooker and season with the herbs.

2. Place the chicken on top of the vegetables and pour over all the stock.

3. Cook for 8 hours.

4. Once ready, shred the chicken meat from the bones.

5. Return the meat to the slow cooker, and season with lemon juice, salt and pepper.

6. Remove the herbs and serve the chicken into bowls with dill or parsley.

7. Serve with crusty bread.

Slow Cooker Duck and Pineapple Curry

Difficulty: Easy ¦ Calories: 659 kcal ¦ Servings: 6
Carbs: 20 g ¦ Protein: 38 g ¦ Fat: 49 g

Ingredients

- 6 duck legs
- 6 kaffir lime leaves
- 1 can coconut milk
- 1 small pineapple, cut into chunks
- 2 tbsp fish sauce
- 2 tbsp light brown sugar
- 1 red chilli
- 4 tbsp red Thai curry paste
- Thai basil leaves, for serving

Preparation

1. Fry the duck legs for about 15 minutes.

2. Once ready, remove the duck from the pan. In the same casserole, cook the sugar in the duck's fat until caramelised.

3. Add in the curry paste, coconut milk and some water. Bring to a simmer, then stir in the lime leaves and fish sauce.

4. Place everything into the slow cooker and cook for 8 hours on high.

5. When it is ready, remove the legs. In the duck's fat, stir in the pineapple, the basil and half the chilli.

6. Cook for a few more minutes, then serves everything together along with some rice.

Slow Cooker Spiced Carrot Lentil Soup

Difficulty: Easy ¦ Calories: 238 kcal ¦ Servings: 4
Carbs: 34 g ¦ Protein: 11 g ¦ Fat: 7 g

Ingredients

- 140 g (5 oz.) red lentils
- 600 g (21 oz.) carrots, grated
- 125 ml (1/2 cup) milk
- 2 tsp cumin seeds
- 2 tbsp olive oil
- Vegetable stock
- Plain yoghurt, to serve
- Naan bread, to serve

Preparation

1. Place the vegetable stock, carrots, lentils, cumin seeds, oil, chilli flakes and cumin seeds into your slow cooker.

2. Cook for 3 hours on high.

3. Fry additional cumin seeds and chilli flakes for a couple of minutes.

4. When the lentils are ready, stir in the milk. You can whizz the soup with a food processor if you want to make it smoother.

5. Serve with fried spices, plain yoghurt, or naan bread.

Slow Cooker Lamb Curry

Difficulty: Easy ¦ Calories: 568 kcal ¦ Servings: 2
Carbs: 49 g ¦ Protein: 43 g ¦ Fat: 19 g

Ingredients

- 425 g (14 oz.) chopped tomatoes
- 25 g (0.8 oz.) red lentils
- 20 g (0.7 oz.) can chickpeas
- 75 g (2.6 oz.) curly kale
- 1 large onion, sliced
- 250 g (8.5 oz.) lean lamb steak, diced
- 2 tsp vegetable bouillon powder
- 3 tbsp Madras curry paste
- 1 cinnamon stick
- 1 tsp cumin seeds
- 1 tbsp grated ginger
- Cooked brown rice, to serve

Preparation

1. Put all the ingredients (except for the rice) into the slow cooker.
2. Cover with water and let rest in the fridge overnight.
3. Stir well and then cook for 6 hours on low.
4. Serve with brown rice.

Slow Cooker Beef Goulash

Difficulty: Easy ¦ Calories: 581 kcal ¦ Servings: 8
Carbs: 17 g ¦ Protein: 54 g ¦ Fat: 32 g

Ingredients

- ◆ 2 kg (4.4 lbs.) stewing steak, cut into chunks
- ◆ 4 mixed peppers, cut into chunks
- ◆ 500 ml (2 cups) beef stock
- ◆ 4 large tomatoes, cut into chunks
- ◆ 2 large onions, chopped
- ◆ 300 ml (1.3 cups) soured cream
- ◆ 3 tbsp olive oil
- ◆ 4 tbsp tomato puree
- ◆ 2 tbsp flour
- ◆ 3 garlic cloves
- ◆ 2 tsp caraway seeds
- ◆ 1 tbsp sweet smoked paprika
- ◆ Parsley, chopped

Preparation

1. Cook the beef in a pan until brown.

2. Use the same oil and pan to fry the onions until golden.

3. Add in garlic and pepper, flour and all of the spices. Cook for 10 minutes.

4. Stir in the tomatoes, and the tomato puree. Bring to simmer while gradually adding the beef stock.

5. Transfer everything into the slow cooker with the seared beef. Cover the meat in stock.

6. Cook for 7 hours on low. Ensure that the sauce has thickened and that the beef is tender.

7. Mix in the soured cream and parsley.

8. Serve with more parsley, sweet smoked paprika and roasted potatoes.

Slow Cooker Buffalo Chicken Chilli

Difficulty: Easy ¦ Calories: 378 kcal ¦ Servings: 6
Carbs: 28 g ¦ Protein: 24 g ¦ Fat: 20 g

Ingredients

- 450 g (1 lb) ground chicken
- 225 g (8 oz) cream cheese
- 425 g (15 oz.) canned white beans
- 425 g (15 oz.) can fire-roasted tomatoes
- 1 cup frozen corn kernels
- ½ tsp garlic powder
- ½ tsp dried cilantro
- ½ tsp celery salt
- ½ tsp onion powder
- 1 package ranch dressing mix
- ¼ cup buffalo wing sauce
- 1 l (2 cups) chicken broth
- Crumbled blue cheese, to serve (optional)

Preparation

1. Cook the chicken until browned, then transfer into the slow cooker.

2. Add all the remaining ingredients.

3. Top with cream cheese.

4. Cook for 8 hours (or 4 hours on low).

5. Once ready, incorporate more cream cheese and additional wing sauce, if needed.

6. Serve with blue cheese crumbles.

Slow Cooker Paella

. . . .

Difficulty: Medium ¦ Calories: 517 kcal ¦ Servings: 4
Carbs: 46 g ¦ Protein: 31 g ¦ Fat: 21 g

Ingredients

- 240 g (8.5 oz.) chorizo, sliced
- 400 g (14 oz.) chopped tomatoes
- 300 g (19.5 oz.) paella rice
- 400 ml (1.7 cups) chicken stock
- 150 ml (0.6 cups) white wine
- 150 g (5.3 oz.) frozen peas
- 200 g (7 oz.) raw king prawns
- Fresh parsley, chopped
- 2 garlic cloves
- 1 onion, sliced
- 4 boneless, skinless chicken thighs, sliced
- 2 tbsp olive oil
- 1 tbsp sweet smoked paprika
- A pinch of saffron (optional)
- Lemon wedges, to serve
- Bread, to serve

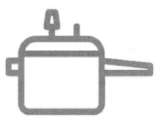

Preparation

1. Fry the chorizo and the chicken for 10 minutes in olive oil.

2. Transfer to the slow cooker.

3. In the same pan, cook the onion for about 5 minutes.

4. Stir in the paprika, garlic and saffron and cook for another couple of minutes.

5. Pour in the wine and simmer until reduced.

6. Pour into the slow cooker.

7. Add in the tomatoes, stock, and rice.

8. Cook for 1 ½ hour.

9. Add the prawns and the peas and cook for another ½ hour or until the rice is ready.

10. Serve with lemon wedges and/or crusty bread.

Slow Cooker Sweet and Spicy Maple Vegan Meatballs

Difficulty: Medium ¦ Calories: 396 kcal ¦ Servings: 6
Carbs: 34 g ¦ Protein: 12 g ¦ Fat: 12 g

Ingredients

- 560 g (20 oz.) can diced pineapple
- 450 g (16 oz.) frozen vegan meatballs
- 1 cup tomato sauce
- ½ white onion, chopped
- 1 green bell pepper, chopped
- 1 red bell pepper, chopped
- 2 tbsp cornstarch
- 2 jalapeno peppers
- 1/3 cup pineapple juice
- ½ cup maple syrup
- ½ tsp garlic powder
- ¼ ground ginger
- Cooked rice, to serve

Preparation

1. Cook the onion in olive oil for about 10 minutes.

2. Add in the bell peppers and jalapeno peppers.

3. Combine the cornstarch, pineapple juice, tomato sauce, maple syrup, garlic powder, and ginger in a small bowl. Stir well.

4. Pour the pineapple juice mixture onto the pepper mixture.

5. Add in the diced pineapple and frozen meatballs.

6. Cook for 6 hours on low (or 3 hours on high).

7. Serve with rice.

Slow Cooker Shepard Pie

Difficulty: Medium ¦ Calories: 438 kcal ¦ Servings: 4
Carbs: 57 g ¦ Protein: 23 g ¦ Fat: 10 g

Ingredients

- 250 g (8.8 oz) lean minced lamb or beef
- 400 g (14 oz.) lentils, or white bean
- 2 carrots, diced
- 1 onion, chopped

- 1 tbsp olive oil
- 1 tbsp plain flour
- 1 tsp Worcestershire sauce
- 1 tbsp tomato puree
- 3 thyme sprigs

Toppings

- 250 g (8.8 oz.) sweet potatoes, cut into chunks
- 650 g (23 oz.) potatoes, cut into chunks
- 2 tbsp half-fat crème Fraiche

Preparation

1. Fry the thyme sprigs and the onion in olive oil.

2. Add the carrot and the mince, and cook for 2 minutes, or until no longer pink.

3. Add the flour and the tomato sauce and keep cooking.

4. Finally, stir in the lentils and season with Worcestershire sauce, salt and pepper. Add a bit of water, if necessary.

5. Transfer everything into the slow cooker.

6. Cook all the potatoes in boiling water for about 15 minutes.

7. Once ready, mash them with the crème Fraiche.

8. Scoop this mixture over the mince and cook everything for 5 hours on low.

Slow Cooker Spicy Spaghetti with Garlic Mushrooms

Difficulty: Medium ¦ Calories: 346 kcal ¦ Servings: 4
Carbs: 12 g ¦ Protein: 12 g ¦ Fat: 7 g

Ingredients

- 400 g (14 oz.) chopped tomatoes
- 250 g (8.8 oz.) chestnut mushrooms, sliced
- 300 g (10.5 oz.) spaghetti
- 1 onion, chipped
- 1 celery stick, chopped
- 2 tbsp olive oil
- ½ red chilli
- Parsley leaves only
- 1 garlic clove

Preparation

1. Fry the mushrooms in olive oil for 4 minutes.

2. Add the garlic and cook for another minute, then transfer to a bowl along with the parsley.

3. In the same saucepan, fry the celery and onion for 5 minutes.

4. Transfer all the ingredients (except for the spaghetti) in the slow cooker and cook for 6 hours on low.

5. Cook the spaghetti in boiling water.

6. Mix the spaghetti with the mushroom mix and serve with fresh parsley.

Slow Cooker Turkish Lamb Pilau

Difficulty: Medium ¦ Calories: 584 kcal ¦ Servings: 4
Carbs: 65 g ¦ Protein: 32 g ¦ Fat: 24 g

Ingredients

- 500 g (17 oz.) lean lamb neck fillet, cubed
- 1 large onion, sliced
- 250 g (9 oz.) basmati rice
- Vegetable stock
- 2 cinnamon sticks
- 12 dried apricots
- Pine nuts or flaked almonds
- 1 tbsp olive oil
- Fresh mint leaves, chopped

Preparation

1. Fry the pine nuts or almonds in olive oil.

2. Add in the cinnamon and onion, and stir well.

3. Stir in the lamb and cook until browned.

4. Add the rice and cook for 2 more minutes.

5. Transfer everything in the slow cooker and cook for 4 hours on low.

6. Pour the vegetable stock in boiling water along with the apricots.

7. When everything is ready, garnish with additional pine nuts and mint leaves before serving.

Slow Cooker Pulled Pork

....

Difficulty: Medium ¦ Calories: 150 kcal ¦ Servings: 12
Carbs: 3 g ¦ Protein: 18 g ¦ Fat: 6 g

Ingredients

- 1.8 kg (4 lbs.) pork shoulder
- ¼ cup apple cider vinegar
- 1 tsp cayenne pepper
- 1 tsp pepper
- 2 tbsp brown sugar

- 1 tsp onion powder
- 1 tsp garlic powder
- 2 tbsp paprika
- ¾ cup of water

Preparation

1. Mix all the powdered spices and rub into the pork.

2. Place water and vinegar in the bottom of your slow cooker.

3. Place the pork. Be careful and try not to wash off all the spices!

4. Cook for about 8 hours on low.

Slow Cooker Vegan Red Curry

Difficulty: Medium ¦ Calories: 510 kcal ¦ Servings: 4
Carbs: 17 g ¦ Protein: 15 g ¦ Fat: 19 g

Ingredients

- 4 scallions, chopped
- 2 tbsp red curry paste
- 1 green bell pepper, sliced
- 1 red bell pepper, sliced
- 1 cup full-fat coconut milk
- 1 tbsp soy sauce
- 1 tbsp fresh ginger
- 2 cups chickpeas
- 1 tbsp maple syrup
- 1 cup sliced carrots
- 2 cups vegetable broth
- ½ tbsp peanut butter
- 1/3 cup Thai basil
- 1 tbsp fresh lime juice
- 1 Thai chilli
- ¾ cup of rice

Preparation

1. Whisk together the coconut milk, peanut butter, and red curry paste. Transfer into the slow cooker with the rest of the ingredients.

2. Cook for 6 hours on low.

3. Stir in the rice and cook for other 45 minutes.

4. Serve with Thai basil while still hot.

Slow Cooker Vegan BBQ Jackfruit Tacos

Difficulty: Medium ¦ Calories: 442 kcal ¦ Servings: 6 tacos
Carbs: 80 g ¦ Protein: 10 g ¦ Fat: 12 g

Ingredients

BBQ Jackfruit

- 2 x 550 g (20 oz.) cans green jackfruit (in brine)
- 1 tbsp sriracha
- 2/3 cup BBQ sauce
- 1 red onion, diced
- 3 tbsp tomato paste
- 1 tbsp ground cumin
- 1 tsp lemon juice
- 1 tsp smoked paprika
- ¾ cup vegetable stock

Avocado Cream

- 1 ripe avocado
- ½ cup of water
- The juice of 1 lemon
- 1 tsp crushed garlic
- 2 tbsp extra-virgin olive oil
- Salt and pepper
- Fresh cilantro

To assemble and serve

- Chopped red onion
- Shredded lettuce
- Chopped tomatoes
- Taco shells
- Any additional toppings of your choice

Preparation

1. Drain the jackfruit cans, then cut the hard tips of each fruit.

2. Add the jackfruits into the slow cooker, along with garlic, onion, smoked paprika, cumin. Season with salt and pepper.

3. Once the jackfruits are completely covered with spices, add the tomato paste, BBQ sauce, lemon juice, sriracha, and vegetable stock.

4. Stir to mix everything.

5. Cook on low for about 6 hours.

6. Meanwhile, to make the avocado cream, add all the ingredients to a food processor and blend until you get a creamy mixture.

7. Once the jackfruits are ready, you can finally assemble the tacos! Layer the jackfruit mixture, the avocado cream, and all other ingredients over a taco shell or a soft tortilla.

Slow Cooker Lentil Sloppy Joes

Difficulty: Medium ¦ Calories: 468 kcal ¦ Servings: 4
Carbs: 80 g ¦ Protein: 15 g ¦ Fat: 9 g

Ingredients

Sloppy Joes

- 425 g (15 oz.) can diced tomatoes
- 2 cups vegetable broth
- 1 cup brown lentils
- 1 red bell pepper, chopped
- 1 medium onion, chopped
- 2 tbsp tomato paste
- 2 cloves garlic, minced
- 1 tbsp maple syrup
- 1 tsp chilli powder
- 1 tbsp Dijon mustard
- 1 tsp cumin
- 1 tsp fresh lemon juice
- 1 tsp smoked paprika
- 1 tsp soy sauce
- Salt and pepper

Coleslaw

- ½ tsp celery salt
- 1 tsp apple cider vinegar
- ¼ cup vegan mayonnaise
- 2 ½ cups shredded cabbage
- Hamburger buns

Preparation

1. Add all the sloppy joe ingredients into the cook slower. Mix everything.

2. Cook for 3 ½ hours on high. If necessary, add more water until completely cooked.

3. Meanwhile, you can start making the coleslaw. Combine all the ingredients in a bowl and refrigerate.

4. When everything is ready, you can serve the lentil sloppy joe on fresh hamburger buns with your coleslaw.

Slow Cooker Vegetable Chowder

Difficulty: Medium ¦ Calories: 368 kcal ¦ Servings: 4
Carbs: 80 g ¦ Protein: 25 g ¦ Fat: 19 g

Ingredients

- 1 bell pepper, chopped
- 3 cups vegetable broth
- ½ cup onion, chopped
- 2 cups fresh green beans, chopped
- 1 carrot, chopped
- 2 cups potatoes, chopped
- 425 g (15 oz.) can creamed corn
- 1 tsp dried oregano
- 1 tsp dried basil
- 2 tbsp cornstarch
- 1 tsp dried parsley
- 1 cup of soy milk

Preparation

1. Place the celery, corn, potatoes, onion, pepper, carrots, green beans, broth, basil, oregano and parsley into the slow cooker.

2. Cook on low for 6 hours, or 4 hours on high. The potatoes must be tender.

3. Season with salt and pepper and add more broth, if necessary.

4. In a separate bowl, whisk together the cornstarch and the soy milk.

5. Pour the mixture over the potatoes and cook for another 1/2 hour, or until the soy milk sauce is thick.

6. Serve hot.

Slow Cooker Walnut Lentils Tacos

Difficulty: Medium ¦ Calories: 468 kcal ¦ Servings: 12 tacos
Carbs: 80 g ¦ Protein: 35 g ¦ Fat: 49 g

Ingredients

- 1 white onion, diced
- 435 g (15 oz.) can fire-roasted diced tomatoes
- 1 cup dried brown lentils
- 1 tbsp chilli powder
- 1 garlic clove, minced
- 2 ¼ cups vegetable broth
- ¼ tsp oregano
- ¼ tsp red pepper flakes
- ½ tsp paprika
- ½ tsp garlic powder
- Salt and pepper
- ¾ cup chopped walnuts
- Your choice of toppings
- Corn tortillas

Preparation

1. Cook the garlic clove and onion in olive oil until tender, or for about 3 minutes.

2. Add all the spices and stir well.

3. Stir in the tomatoes, walnuts, vegetable broth and lentils.

4. Place all the ingredients into the slow cooker, and cook until the vegetables are ready and the lentil mixture is thick.

5. Serve with corn or flour tortillas, and your choice of toppings.

Slow Cooker Chickpea Tagine

Difficulty: Medium ¦ Calories: 278 kcal ¦ Servings: 4
Carbs: 30 g ¦ Protein: 15 g ¦ Fat: 19 g

Ingredients

♦ 2 carrots, chopped

♦ 1 large onion, chopped

♦ 4 garlic cloves, chopped

♦ 2 tbsp tomato paste

♦ 1 tbsp extra-virgin olive oil

♦ 2 x 400 g (14 oz.) cans chickpeas

♦ 2 x 400 g (14 oz) cans chopped tomatoes

♦ 3 tbsp maple syrup

♦ ½ cup chopped dried apricots

♦ 1 tbsp flour

♦ 1 tsp turmeric

♦ 1 tsp ground cinnamon

♦ 1 tsp ground coriander

♦ 1 tsp ground cumin

♦ Chopped cilantro

♦ 1 tsp cayenne pepper

♦ Fresh ginger, chopped

♦ Cooked couscous, to serve

Preparation

1. Cook the carrots along with the garlic and onions in olive oil for 10 minutes, or until soft.

2. Toss flour and stir well.

3. Add in the maple syrup and tomato paste, and keep stirring.

4. Add in all the spices, herbs and the ginger. Season with salt and pepper and add the chopped tomatoes.

5. Place everything in the slow cooker with the chickpeas and dried apricots.

6. Cook for 4 hours on high.

7. Garnish with chopped cilantro and serve with couscous.

Slow Cooker Butternut Squash and Black Bean Chilli

Difficulty: Medium ¦ Calories: 318 kcal ¦ Servings: 8
Carbs: 15 g ¦ Protein: 29 g ¦ Fat: 19 g

Ingredients

- 2 jalapenos
- 4 cups chopped butternut squash
- 2 garlic cloves, minced
- 1 cup red onion, chopped
- 1 green pepper, chopped
- 500 ml (2 cups) vegetable broth
- 800 g (28 oz.) can diced tomatoes
- 2 x 425 g (15 oz.) cans bleak bean
- 1 tbsp olive oil
- 1 tbsp balsamic vinegar
- 1 tbsp chilli powder
- 1 tsp cumin
- ¼ tsp cayenne pepper
- Chilli (optional)

Preparation

1. Cook the onion in olive oil until tender. Stir in the garlic, chopped bell pepper and jalapeno. Cook for a few minutes.

2. Stir in the balsamic vinegar.

3. Add everything to the slow cooker.

4. Mix in the chilli powder, cayenne, cinnamon, black beans, cumin, vegetable broth, butternut squash, and tomatoes.

5. Cook for 6 hours on high.

6. Add all the remaining ingredients to the onion mixture once ready, then bring to a simmer in a saucepan for another hour.

Slow Cooker Spicy Chicken Chili with Beer Biscuits

Difficulty: Medium ¦ Calories: 275 kcal ¦ Servings: 4
Carbs: 31 g ¦ Protein: 11 g ¦ Fat: 13 g

Ingredients

- 800 g (28 oz) fire-roasted crushed tomatoes
- 1 tsp chipotle chilli powder
- 1 tsp cumin
- 1 tsp roasted garlic powder
- 3 tsp ancho chilli powder

- 250 ml (1 cup) chicken broth
- 1 tsp olive oil
- 400 g (14 oz.) ground chicken
- ½ tsp Mexican oregano
- ½ tsp dried cilantro

Biscuits

- 5 tsp butter
- 250 ml (1 cup) beer
- 1 ¾ cups all-purpose flour
- 400 g (1 cup) shredded cheddar cheese
- 1 tsp baking powder
- A pinch of salt

Preparation

1. Brown the chicken in olive oil. Once ready, shred the meat from the bones.

2. Transfer to slow cooker with remaining ingredients.

3. Cook on 8 hours on high (or 4 hours on low).

4. To make the biscuits, mix baking powder, flour and salt into a small bowl.

5. Cut the cold butter into small cubes and add into the flour mixture. Stir in the cheese.

6. Drop a few spoonsful of this mixture onto parchment paper.

7. Bake at 200 C (400 F) for 10 minutes.

8. Serve the chicken with shredded cheese and the beer biscuits.

Slow Cooker Pot Roast with Gravy

Difficulty: Medium ¦ Calories: 547 kcal ¦ Servings: 5
Carbs: 34 g ¦ Protein: 40 g ¦ Fat: 26 g

Ingredients

- 900 g (2 lbs.) chuck roast
- 225 g (8 oz.) baby carrots
- ¼ cup tapioca pearls
- 3 cups beef broth
- 1 tbsp olive oil
- 1 tbsp herb and garlic seasoning
- 2 cloves garlic
- 450 g (16 oz.) potatoes, halved
- 2 tbsp tomato paste
- ¼ cup cornstarch
- ½ cup red wine
- 1 tbsp butter
- 1 tbsp olive oil

Preparation

1. Season the roast with the herb and garlic seasoning.

2. Cook the roast on both sides in olive oil, then transfer it to the slow cooker.

3. Add carrots and potatoes.

4. Whisk the cornstarch with water until smooth.

5. Pour the mixture over the roast, together with all the remaining ingredients.

6. Cook for 10 hours on low or until well tender.

Slow Cooker Quinoa Enchiladas

Difficulty: Challenging ¦ Calories: 432 kcal ¦ Servings: 6
Carbs: 56 g ¦ Protein: 17 g ¦ Fat: 16 g

Ingredients

Enchilada Sauce

- 1 cup vegetable broth
- 425 g (15 oz.) can crushed tomatoes
- 1 tsp chilli powder
- 3 tbsp oil
- 1/8 tsp cinnamon
- ½ tsp garlic powder
- 1 ½ tsp cumin
- ½ tsp oregano
- 3 tbsp all-purpose flour
- ¼ tsp cayenne pepper
- Salt

Enchilada

- 1 medium zucchini, chopped
- ¾ cup of water
- 425 g (can black beans)
- 115 g (4 oz.) can diced jalapenos
- 425 g (can corn)
- 2 bell peppers
- 1 medium onion
- 1 cup uncooked quinoa
- 4 corn tortillas
- ¼ cup fresh cilantro
- 1 cup shredded cheddar cheese
- 4 corn tortillas, to serve

Preparation

1. Start by making the enchilada sauce. Cook the flour for 3-4 minutes in olive oil.

2. Add all the remaining spices and stir well for a few minutes.

3. Add in the crushed tomatoes and some water. Keep cooking until you get a thick sauce. Remove 1 cup of this mixture and set aside for later.

4. Add the onion, bell peppers, and zucchini into the slow cooker. Drizzle with olive oil and cook until the vegetables are ready.

5. Add in the quinoa and keep cooking until ready. It should take about 6 hours to cook all the ingredients together.

6. Once ready, stir in the cheese, cilantro, jalapeno, corn, and black beans.

7. Serve hot, with corn tortillas and the extra enchilada sauce.

Bonus: Slow Cooker Indian Recipes

Slow Cooker Indian Spiced Lentils

....

Difficulty: Easy ¦ Calories: 365 kcal ¦ Servings: 12
Carbs: 34 g ¦ Protein: 57 g ¦ Fat: 12 g

Ingredients

- ♦ 4 serrano chiles
- ♦ 800 g (28 oz.) can diced tomatoes
- ♦ 1 large onion
- ♦ 750 g (3 cups) red or yellow lentils
- ♦ ¼ cup cilantro leaves
- ♦ 2 tbsp ground cumin
- ♦ 2 tbsp curry powder
- ♦ 2 tsp ground turmeric
- ♦ ½ tsp granulated sugar
- ♦ 1 tsp chilli powder
- ♦ 5 cloves garlic
- ♦ 400 g (14 oz.) heavy cream
- ♦ Basmati rice or naan, to serve
- ♦ Lemon juice, to serve

Preparation

1. Soak the lentils for about 10 minutes, then drain and rinse well before transferring them to the slow cooker.

2. In a food processor, combine the chopped onion, ginger, garlic, curry powder, serrano chiles, cumin, chilli powder, turmeric, and sugar. Process until you obtain a thick paste.

3. Transfer this mixture to the slow cooker with the diced tomatoes and some water.

4. Cook all the ingredients for 4 hours (or 8 hours on low).

5. When the lentils are soft and ready, you can adjust the seasonings to taste.

6. Smash half of the lentils with a spoon. To make the texture creamier, you can stir in the heavy cream or some butter.

7. Serve warm with lemon juice, and basmati rice or warm naan bread.

Slow Cooker Chicken Tikka Masala

Difficulty: Medium ¦ Calories: 325 kcal ¦ Servings: 6
Carbs: 8 g ¦ Protein: 34 g ¦ Fat: 17 g

Ingredients

- 900 g (2 lbs.) chicken breasts
- 2 medium yellow onions
- 2 tbsp oil
- 500 ml (2 cups) tomato puree
- 1 tbsp lemon juice

- 1 tbsp Kashmiri red chilli powder
- 3 tbsp plain yoghurt
- ½ tsp garam masala
- 1 tbsp garlic
- 1 tbsp grated ginger

Garnish

- 125 ml (1/2 cup) heavy cream
- Fresh cilantro (chopped)
- 1 tbsp tomato paste
- 2 tbsp dried fenugreek leaves

Preparation

1. Cut the chicken breasts into cubes. Season with salt and lemon juice.

2. Add yoghurt, turmeric, ginger, garlic, red chilli powder, and garam masala. Mix well and leave the meat to marinate while you prepare the remaining ingredients.

3. Fry the onions in olive oil until they turn translucent.

4. Spread the onion evenly in the slow cooker. Add a layer of tomato puree.

5. Spread the spiced chicken cubes over the tomato puree.

6. Leave to cook in the slow cooker for about 4 hours.

7. Serve with all the garnishing ingredients and mix well.

8. Optionally, add 1 tsp of sugar to balance the flavours of the spices.

Slow Cooker Lentil Curry

. . . .

Difficulty: Easy ¦ Calories: 376 kcal ¦ Servings: 6
Carbs: 36 g ¦ Protein: 14 g ¦ Fat: 20 g

Ingredients

- 1 yellow pepper, diced
- 1 red onion
- 2 tbsp olive oil
- 3 garlic cloves
- 750 g (26 oz.) green lentils
- 1 can full-fat coconut milk
- 1 tsp cumin
- 1 tsp garlic powder
- 3 tbsp tomato paste
- 2 tsp garam masala
- 2 cups of water
- 2 tsp sugar
- Salt and pepper
- Jasmine rice or basmati rice, to serve

Preparation

1. Place the pepper, red onion, and minced garlic in the slow cooker. Pour the olive oil.

2. Rinse the lentils and add them to the slow cooker.

3. Stir well, then add all the remaining ingredients and stir again.

4. Cook on low for 4 hours. Make sure it doesn't need more water while it cooks.

5. Serve with your choice of rice.

Slow Cooker Indian Chicken Curry

Difficulty: Medium ¦ Calories: 485 kcal ¦ Servings: 6
Carbs: 38 g ¦ Protein: 39 g ¦ Fat: 37 g

Ingredients

- 800 g (2 lbs.) boneless chicken thighs
- 2 cloves garlic
- ¾ tsp curry powder
- 1 ½ tsp turmeric
- 1 ½ tsp cumin
- ½ tbsp cornstarch
- 125 ml (1/2 cup) chicken stock
- 225 g (8 oz.) tomato puree
- ½ large yellow onion, diced
- 1 tbsp + ½ tsp garam masala
- ¾ cup plain Greek yoghurt
- 250 ml (1 cup) half and half cream
- ½ tsp cayenne pepper

Preparation

1. Stir together the garlic, ginger, onions, tomato puree, chicken stock, lemon juice and yoghurt in a mixing bowl. Add the remaining spices and stir well.

2. Place the chicken thighs, cut into pieces, into the slow cooker. Pour the spice mixture on top and stir well to combine.

3. Add some bay leaves and cook on low heat for 8 hours.

4. Meanwhile, mix the half and half cream with the cornstarch. Pour this mixture over the chicken about 30 minutes before it is ready with more garam masala if needed.

5. When the chicken breasts are ready, you can serve them with basmati rice. Remember to remove bay leaves before serving.

Slow Cooker Butter Chickpeas

Difficulty: Easy ¦ Calories: 523 kcal ¦ Servings: 4
Carbs: 44 g ¦ Protein: 19 g ¦ Fat: 37 g

Ingredients

- 350 g (12 oz.) firm tofu
- 420 g (15 oz.) garbanzo beans
- 4 garlic cloves
- 1 can coconut milk
- 1 cup tomato puree
- 1 medium-size onion, diced
- 2 tsp chilli powder
- 1 tbsp olive oil
- 1 tbsp + 1 tsp curry powder
- 1 tbsp + 1 tsp garam masala
- ½ tsp ground ginger
- Salt and pepper

Preparation

1. Rinse the tofu in a paper towel, and allow it to drain out for about 15 minutes.

2. Meanwhile, cook the onion with olive oil in a saucepan. Add the garlic and stir well.

3. Whisk in the tomato puree, curry powder, coconut milk, garam masala, ground ginger and chilli powder. Season with salt and pepper. Cook for about 5 minutes.

4. Cut the tofu and place it into your slow cooker, along with the garbanzo beans.

5. Pour the sauce on top.

6. Cook for 5 hours or until smooth and thick.

7. Garnish with cilantro and serve with naan or rice.

Slow Cooker Butternut Squash Lentil Curry

Difficulty: Easy ¦ Calories: 286 kcal ¦ Servings: 8
Carbs: 34 g ¦ Protein: 12 g ¦ Fat: 12 g

Ingredients

- 2 cups dried red lentils
- (19 oz.) diced tomatoes
- (13.5 oz.) coconut milk
- 4 cups butternut squash
- 2 cloves garlic
- 700 ml (3 cups) stock
- 2 tsp garam masala
- 2 tsp ground cumin

- 2 tsp turmeric
- 1 tbsp curry powder
- 1 onion
- 2 tsp ground coriander
- 2 tbsp fresh ginger
- Salt and pepper
- ½ lime juice

Preparation

1. Combine all ingredients (except for lime juice) and place into your slow cooker.

2. Cook for 8 hours on low.

3. Once ready, season with lime, salt and pepper.

4. Mash everything up until you get a smooth puree and serve with warm naan bread.

Slow Cooker Chickpea Curry

Difficulty: Easy ¦ Calories: 416 kcal ¦ Servings: 6
Carbs: 39 g ¦ Protein: 9 g ¦ Fat: 25 g

Ingredients

- 800 g (28 oz.) chickpeas, drained
- 400 g (14 oz.) sweet potatoes, chopped
- 1 large onion
- 350 g (1 ½ cup) heavy cream or unsweetened coconut milk
- 4 cloves garlic
- 2 tsp ground cumin
- 2 tsp ground turmeric
- 1 tbsp honey
- 2 tsp garam masala
- ½ tsp crushed red pepper
- 1 tbsp fresh ginger, grated
- Basmati rice or naan bread, to serve

Preparation

1. Fry the onions, garlic and ginger in olive oil for 5 minutes.

2. Place this mixture in a blender, and add the cream, honey and all spices. Puree until smooth.

3. Pour this blend into your slow cooker.

4. Add the chickpeas and sweet potatoes.

5. Cook for 8 hours (or 4 hours on high).

6. Serve with basmati rice or naan bread.

Slow Cooker Spicy Chicken Curry

···

Difficulty: Medium ¦ Calories: 386 kcal ¦ Servings: 4
Carbs: 16 g ¦ Protein: 22 g ¦ Fat: 28 g

Ingredients

- 3 chicken breasts
- 1 piece of ginger
- 3 cloves garlic
- 1 large onion
- 3 tsp hot chilli powder
- Salt and pepper
- 1 tbsp vegetable oil
- 1 tsp paprika
- 1 tbsp curry powder
- 1 tbsp ground coriander
- 1 tsp cinnamon
- ½ tbsp cumin
- 240 ml (1 cup) chicken stock
- 2 tbsp tomato puree
- 400 g (14 oz.) tinned chopped tomatoes
- 400 ml (14 oz.) full-fat coconut milk

- 2 tsp sugar
- Chopped coriander or cilantro, to serve
- Boiled rice or naan bread, to serve

Preparation

1. Fry the onion in vegetable oil for 5 minutes, or until softened.

2. Add the diced chicken breasts and cook for a few minutes.

3. Add in all the spices and season with salt and pepper.

4. Cook for another couple of minutes, then add in the chicken stock, coconut milk, tomato puree, tinned tomatoes. Add a pinch of sugar to adjust the acidity of the tomato puree.

5. Bring to the boil, then pour everything into the slow cooker. Cook for 5 hours (or 3 hours on high).

6. Serve with sprinkled fresh coriander or cilantro, and rice or naan.

Slow Cooker Vegan Tikka Masala

Difficulty: Medium ¦ Calories: 286 kcal ¦ Servings: 6
Carbs: 22 g ¦ Protein: 11 g ¦ Fat: 17 g

Ingredients

- ◆ 400 g (14 oz.) firm tofu, drained and cubed
- ◆ 425 g (15 oz.) garbanzo beans
- ◆ 425 g (15 oz.) tomato sauce
- ◆ 4 garlic cloves
- ◆ 1 large onion, chopped
- ◆ 2 tsp ground coriander
- ◆ 1 tbsp garam masala
- ◆ ¼ tsp ground cinnamon
- ◆ 1 tsp ground turmeric
- ◆ 2 tsp smoked paprika
- ◆ ½ tsp ground cayenne pepper
- ◆ 2 tbsp olive oil
- ◆ 1 bay leaf
- ◆ 2 tbsp freshly grated ginger
- ◆ 1 cup full-fat canned coconut milk
- ◆ ½ lemon juice
- ◆ 2 tbsp cornstarch
- ◆ Cooked basmati rice, to serve

Preparation

1. Grease your slow cooker basket with some olive oil.

2. Combine all the spices and tomato sauce.

3. Place the chickpeas and tofu into the slow cooker, then pour the spices mixture on top. Top with the bay leaf.

4. Cook for 8 hours (or 4 hours on high).

5. In a small bowl, mix the coconut milk with the cornstarch and mix well.

6. Add this mixture into the slow cooker once the chickpeas and tofu are ready, and cook for an additional ½ hour, or until thickened.

7. Once ready, add the lemon juice and serve with steamed rice.

Slow Cooker Vegan Saag Paneer

Difficulty: Medium ¦ Calories: 290 kcal ¦ Servings: 6
Carbs: 36 g ¦ Protein: 12 g ¦ Fat: 11 g

Ingredients

- 900 g (2 lbs.) chopped spinach
- 400 ml (14 oz.) full-fat coconut milk
- 400 g (14 oz.) extra-firm tofu, drained
- 5 garlic cloves
- 1 onion, chopped
- 1 Thai chilli, chopped
- 2 tbsp garam masala
- 1 tbsp ground cumin
- 2 tsp cornstarch
- 1 tsp mustard seeds
- 1 tbsp ground cumin
- 1 tbsp turmeric
- 1 tbsp cayenne pepper
- 3 tbsp fresh ginger, grated
- Rice or naan bread, to serve

Preparation

1. Cook the onion in olive oil until softened.

2. Add in the ginger, spices, garlic, and Thai chilli. Cook for another couple of minutes.

3. Once ready, place into a food processor along with the frozen spinach leaves. Process until the spinach are chopped.

4. Place this mixture into the slow cooker along with tomato sauce and coconut milk. Add a pinch of salt and cook for 6 hours on low (or 4 hours on high).

5. Meanwhile, dice the tofu and toss with the cornstarch. Cook in a bit of olive oil.

6. Serve your spinach mixture with tofu, rice or naan bread.

Slow Cooker Indian Beef

Difficulty: Medium ¦ Calories: 627 kcal ¦ Servings: 4
Carbs: 78 g ¦ Protein:57 g ¦ Fat: 35.5 g

Ingredients

- ¼ cup plain flour
- 2 tbsp vegetable oil
- 1 red chilli, chopped
- Fresh ginger, grated
- 800 g (28 oz.) diced beef steak
- 2 garlic cloves
- 1 large brown onion
- ¼ cup curry paste
- 400 g (14 oz.) diced tomatoes
- 2 cardamom pods
- 1 cinnamon stick
- 125 ml (1/2 cup) fresh coriander leaves
- Naan bread, to serve

Preparation

1. Mix the flour and the beef in a snap-lock bag, then season with salt and pepper.

2. Seal the bag and cook in olive oil until browned. When ready, transfer to the slow cooker.

3. In the same pan, cook the onion and garlic, with the ginger.

4. Add chilli and curry paste and stir well for one minute.

5. Add tomatoes and some cold water, then bring to the boil.

6. When the sauce is ready, transfer it to slow cooker.

7. Season with cinnamon and cardamom, then cover and leave to cook for 5 ½ hours.

8. Remove cinnamon and cardamom pods before serving.

9. Sprinkle with some more fresh coriander and serve with warm naan bread.

Slow Cooker Paneer Makhani

Difficulty: Medium ¦ Calories: 618 kcal ¦ Servings: 4
Carbs: 21 g ¦ Protein: 21 g ¦ Fat: 51 g

Ingredients

- 450 g (16 oz.) paneer
- 800 g (28 oz.) crushed tomatoes
- 1 tsp garam masala
- 1 tsp lemon juice
- 1 tsp chilli powder
- 1 tsp cumin
- 1 tsp jarred minced ginger
- ¼ tsp cayenne pepper
- 2 tsp minced garlic
- 75 ml (1/4 cup) diced white onion
- 250 ml (1 cup) heavy cream
- 1 bay leaf
- 75 ml (1/4 cup) plain yoghurt

Preparation

1. Place all the ingredient except for the heavy cream, yoghurt, and paneer, in the slow cooker.

2. Let cook for about 8 hours (or 4 hours on high).

3. Remove the bay leaf.

4. Add the yoghurt and cream, and stir well.

5. When all the ingredients are combined, add the paneer and let heat for another ½ hour.

6. Stir well and serve with rice or naan.

Slow Cooker Butter Chicken (Murch Makhani)

Difficulty: Medium ¦ Calories: 404 kcal ¦ Servings: 4
Carbs: 15 g ¦ Protein: 37 g ¦ Fat: 22 g

Ingredients

- 6 chicken thighs
- 1 onion
- 1 tbsp chilli powder
- 1 tsp turmeric
- 2 tbsp garam masala
- 1 onion
- 1 tbsp curry powder
- 150 g (5 oz.) tomato puree
- 250 ml (1 cup) coconut milk
- 125 ml (1/2 cup) yoghurt
- 1 tbsp olive oil
- coriander
- 2 tsp sugar
- Salt and pepper

Preparation

1. Heat the chicken breast in the olive oil before transferring them in the slow cooker.

2. Use the same oil to fry the onion, then add the crushed garlic and cook for another minute. When ready, add onion and garlic in the slow cooker with the chicken.

3. Mix the all the spices together in a bowl. Add sugar, salt and pepper.

4. Combine the spices mixture with tomato puree, coconut milk and the yoghurt.

5. Pour this mixture over the chicken breasts and onion and stir well.

6. Cook the chicken meat in the slow cooker for up to six hours.

7. Serve with chopped coriander.

Slow Cooker Dal Makhani

Difficulty: Challenging ¦ Calories: 356 kcal ¦ Servings: 4
Carbs: 34 g ¦ Protein: 14 g ¦ Fat: 17 g

Ingredients

- 1 cup black lentils
- 1 tsp ginger garlic paste
- 2 tsp ghee

- 3 cups of water
- ¼ tsp turmeric powder

To add after slow cooking

- ¾ tsp garam masala
- ¼ tsp dried mango powder
- 2 tbsp butter

- ¼ cup heavy cream
- ¾ cup tomato puree
- ¼ tsp red chilli powder

Tempering

- 2 tsp ghee
- 1 tsp lemon juice
- 3 whole dried red chillies
- 3 garlic cloves, finely chopped

Preparation

1. Wash the lentils and add it to the slow cooker along with the water and turmeric powder. Season with a pinch of salt.

2. Add the ginger garlic paste and the ghee, and stir well.

3. Once everything is mixed, cook for 8 hours on low.

4. When it is ready, mash the dal until you get a smooth puree.

5. Add the red chilli powder and garam masala, and mix well.

6. Add tomato puree and keep stirring.

7. Add the butter and cook the mixture in the slow cooker for 2 more hours.

8. Once ready, add the heavy cream, red chillies and chopped garlic.

9. Add remaining spices and garnish with fresh cilantro.

10. Serve with rice or naan.

Printed in Poland
by Amazon Fulfillment
Poland Sp. z o.o., Wrocław

64752336R00066